ACKNOWLEDGMENTS

This book would not have been possible without God's guidance, strength, and grace. Every prayer, every word, and every inspiration serves as a testament to His faithfulness and love

To my family, your steadfast support and understanding have been my foundation throughout this journey. Thank you for providing me with the time, space, and encouragement to see this project through

To my friends and community who prayed for me, cheered me on, and reminded me of God's purpose in my life—thank you for reflecting His grace

I want to express my heartfelt gratitude to each of you who picks up this book. It means so much to me that you're allowing me to be part of your journey. My sincere hope and prayer are that these pages bring you closer to the peace and strength that only God can provide.

With Grace and Joy,

Whitney Ramos

DEDICATION

To all the incredible women who rise each day, pouring your hearts into everyone around you—often putting your own needs aside—this book is truly for you! May you discover God's grace surrounding you in those quiet moments, and His strength uplifting you when life gets busy

And to the wonderful mothers, daughters, sisters, and friends who continue to show up, even when life feels a bit too much—may you feel His peace, His love, and His boundless faithfulness surrounding you.

GRACE
for the
BUSY SOUL

*Prayers and Scriptures
for Every Season of Life*

WHITNEY RAMOS

A Personal Invitation To

GRACE FOR THE BUSY SOUL

Let me ask you something—when was the last time you truly paused? Not just in body, but in spirit. When did you last allow yourself to slow down and feel God's presence, hear His voice, and simply be with Him? If you're anything like me, life often pulls you in multiple directions at once. There's always something demanding your attention, whether it's tasks to complete, places to visit, or people to care for. Although you wish to devote more time to God, it doesn't always happen. This isn't due to a lack of love for Him, but rather because life feels overwhelmingly busy. I truly relate to this.

That's why I wrote this book—not to add another task to your to-do list, but to be a companion for those moments when you need a breath of fresh air for your soul. It's a gentle reminder that God's grace is right there with you, even in the hustle and bustle. You don't need hours of quiet time to connect with Him; sometimes, all it takes is a willingness to turn your heart toward Him—if only for a moment.

This book is here to help you discover peace, clarity, and strength, even on your busiest days. It's all about meeting God where you are, not where you think you should be.

HOW TO USE THIS BOOK

I totally understand—sometimes life gets busy, and we don't have time for lengthy devotionals. That's why I've made this simple and straightforward, so you can easily pick it up whenever you need a moment of peace.

Each chapter is designed to offer you:

Bible Verse – A short but powerful scripture to help ground your heart in truth.

Prayer – A heartfelt invitation to engage in a meaningful conversation with God, especially during moments when we could all use a little guidance to find the right words on our paths.

Reflection – Here, you will discover uplifting reminders that God sees you, knows you, and is actively working in your life right now.

Takeaway – A significant truth to hold onto throughout your day.

Declaration – An empowering statement to claim your life, as our words truly hold power. You can embrace this day by day or explore a chapter that relates to your experiences. Whether you have just five minutes or a full fifty, whether you're settling into a quiet room or sneaking a moment between your busy tasks, God will meet you right here.

Grace for the Busy Soul is a warm and heartfelt invitation! It's an opportunity to pause, reset, and reconnect your heart with God, especially when life feels a little overwhelming. The beautiful truth is that you don't have to wait for a perfect moment to seek Him. He's already right there with you, right now! So, let's dive in together. Let's invite Him into our day, into our thoughts, and into our hearts. And let's hold onto this reminder—even in the busiest seasons, grace is always within reach!

CONTENTS

Contents

CHAPTER 1

PEACE IN THE CHAOS

When was the last time you felt true peace—not just a moment of calm, but a deep, unshakable peace that carried you through the storm? Or have you been so used to chaos that you don't even recognize peace when it comes?

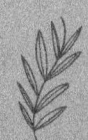

CHAPTER 1

PEACE IN THE CHAOS

*"The Lord will give strength to His people;
the Lord will bless His people with peace."*
Psalm 29:11NKJV

Reflection:

Life doesn't stop for the storms. The deadlines, the responsibilities, the unexpected challenges—they all seem to pile up at once. But in the midst of it all, there is a peace that doesn't depend on the absence of chaos. It comes from God, who is our steady anchor, no matter how rough the waters get.

A PRAYER FOR GRATITUDE

Father, thank You for all that You have given me. Teach me to find joy in the blessings I often overlook. Help me to see Your hand in every detail of my life and to be content, knowing that You provide everything I need. May my heart overflow with thanksgiving every day. In Jesus' name, Amen.

Your Turn: Take a moment to reflect on God's blessings in your life. Write down three things you're grateful for today and why they bring you joy:

_____

_____

_____

_____

_____

_____

_____

_____

Chapter 1: Peace In The Chaos

By Faith, Declare this:

"

I declare that I am content in Christ. I will celebrate His blessings in my life, both seen and unseen. By faith, I choose gratitude over comparison and joy over dissatisfaction.

"

Takeaway: This week, whenever you're tempted to compare or feel dissatisfied, pause and thank God for one blessing in your life.

_____

_____

_____

_____

Chapter 1: Peace In The Chaos

CHAPTER 2

STRENGTH FOR THE JOURNEY

What happens when you feel like you have nothing left to give? Do you push through on empty, pretending you're okay, or do you let God carry you? What if your weakness is actually an invitation to experience His power?

CHAPTER 2

STRENGTH FOR THE JOURNEY

"But those who wait on the Lord shall renew their strength; they shall mount up with wings like eagles, they shall run and not be weary, they shall walk and not faint."
Isaiah 40:31 NKJV

Reflection:

Life's journey can sometimes feel challenging. We all go through seasons of weariness and doubt, and it's natural to feel tempted to give up during tough times. However, God reassures us that He will renew our strength when we choose to wait on Him. His incredible power becomes our own, and His grace lifts us up when we feel overwhelmed. So, take a moment to rest in Him, and let His strength be the fuel that drives you forward on your journey ahead.

A PRAYER FOR STRENGTH

Lord, You are the source of my strength. When I feel weak and weary, remind me that Your power is made perfect in my weakness. Renew my strength as I wait on You, and help me to walk forward in faith, trusting that You are guiding my every step. In Jesus' name, Amen.

Your Turn: Write down one area where you need God's strength:

_____

_____

_____

_____

_____

_____

_____

_____

_____

Chapter 2: Strength for the Journey

By Faith, Declare this:

"

I declare that God's strength is my strength. I will not grow weary because He renews me daily. By faith, I will walk forward, knowing that He is with me every step of the way.

"

Takeaway: When you feel weary this week, pause and remember God's promise: He will renew your strength as you wait on Him.

Chapter 2: Strength for the Journey

CHAPTER 3

GRATITUDE AND CONTENTMENT

Do you find yourself waiting for the next big thingto feel fulfilled? What if what you have right now is exactly what God wants to use to bless you? Could it be that your next breakthrough is locked inside the gratitude you've been withholding?

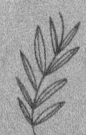

CHAPTER 3

GRATITUDE AND CONTENTMENT

"Now godliness with contentment is great gain. For we brought nothing into this world, and it is certain we can carry nothing out."
1 Timothy 6:6–7 NKJV

In a world that often pushes us to want more, God invites us to rest in gratitude and contentment. Recognizing His blessings, both big and small, allows us to experience the joy of knowing that what we have is already enough. Gratitude shifts our focus from what we lack to the abundance of God's provision in our lives.

15

A PRAYER FOR GRATITUDE

Father, thank You for all that You have given me. Teach me to find joy in the blessings I often overlook. Help me to see Your hand in every detail of my life and to be content, knowing that You provide everything I need. May my heart overflow with thanksgiving every day. In Jesus' name, Amen.

Your Turn: Take a moment to reflect on God's blessings in your life. Write down three things you're grateful for today and why they bring you joy:

_____

_____

_____

_____

_____

_____

_____

_____

Chapter 3: Gratitude and Contentment

By Faith, Declare this:

"

I declare that I am content in Christ. I will celebrate His blessings in my life, both seen and unseen. By faith, I choose gratitude over comparison and joy over dissatisfaction.

"

Takeaway: This week, whenever you're tempted to compare or feel dissatisfied, pause and thank God for one blessing in your life.

_____

_____

_____

_____

18

Chapter 3: Gratitude and Contentment

CHAPTER 4

OVERCOMING ANXIETY AND FEAR

What thoughts have been keeping you up at night? Are they from God, or have you unknowingly allowed the enemy to rent space in your mind? What would your life look like if you fully believed that God is fighting for you?

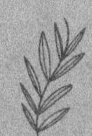

CHAPTER 4

OVERCOMING ANXIETY AND FEAR

"Be anxious for nothing, but in everything by prayer and supplication, with thanksgiving, let your requests be made known to God; and the peace of God, which surpasses all understanding, will guard your hearts and minds through Christ Jesus."
Philippians 4:6-7 NKJV

Reflection:

Anxiety and fear have a way of creeping into our hearts, stealing our peace, and shaking our faith. But God's Word reminds us that we don't have to carry these burdens alone. Through prayer, we can release our worries to Him and receive His peace that guards our hearts and minds. Let go of fear and cling to the promises of His unfailing love.

A PRAYER FOR OVERCOMING ANXIETY

Father, I come to You with every worry and fear that weighs me down. You said to cast my cares on You because You care for me. Replace my anxiety with Your peace, which surpasses all understanding. Help me to trust that You are in control and working all things for my good. In Jesus' name, Amen.

Your Turn: Think of one specific *fear* or *worry* that has been weighing on your heart.
Write it down and then cross it out as a symbol of giving it to God. Write what you will trust Him to do in its place:

Fear:

_____

_____

_____

_____

_____

_____

Trusting God for....

_____

_____

_____

_____

_____

_____

_____

_____

_____

_____

_____

_____

_____

_____

_____

_____

_____

_____

By Faith, Declare this:

"

I declare that fear has no hold on me. God's peace guards my heart and mind. By faith, I will walk boldly, knowing that He is my protector and provider.

"

Takeaway: This week, when fear arises, pause and declare:
"God's peace is my shield, and I will not be shaken."

Chapter 4: Overcoming Anxiety and Fear

CHAPTER 5

RENEWAL AND REST

When was the last time you truly rested—**not just physically, but spiritually? Do you see rest as a weakness or as an act of trust in God? What if slowing down is the key to hearing His voice again?

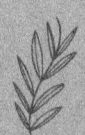

CHAPTER 5

RENEWAL
AND REST

"Come to Me, all you who labor and are heavy laden, and I will give you rest. Take My yoke upon you and learn from Me, for I am gentle and lowly in heart, and you will find rest for your souls."
Matthew 11:28-29 NKJV

Reflection:

We often carry more than we were ever meant to bear, pushing ourselves until we feel drained and empty. But Jesus offers a different way—a promise of rest and renewal for our weary souls. His rest isn't just physical; it's a deep, spiritual renewal that refreshes our hearts and minds. Take His yoke and let Him carry your burdens today.

A PRAYER FOR RENEWAL

Lord, I come to You, weary and in need of rest. You said to cast my burdens on You, for You care for me. Renew my strength, refresh my spirit, and help me to find rest in Your presence. Teach me to trust You and lean on Your grace. In Jesus' name, Amen.

Your Turn: What is one burden you've been carrying for too long? Write it down and then ask God to renew your heart as you give it to Him:

Burden:

_____

_____

_____

_____

_____

_____

_____

Trusting God for:

By Faith, Declare this:

"

I declare that I am renewed and refreshed in Christ. I will not carry burdens I was never meant to bear. By faith, I find rest and restoration in Him.

"

Takeaway: This week, whenever you feel overwhelmed, pause and repeat:
"God is my rest, my renewal, and my strength."

Chapter 5: Renewal and Rest

CHAPTER 6

FAITH AND TRUST IN GOD

Have you been waiting to see it before you believe it? What if faith isn't about seeing the whole path, but about trusting the One who holds it? Would you take the next step if all God gave you was His word?

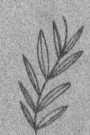

CHAPTER 6

FAITH AND TRUST IN GOD

"Trust in the Lord with all your heart, and lean not on your own understanding; in all your ways acknowledge Him, and He shall direct your paths."
Proverbs 3:5-6 NKJV

Reflection:

Trusting God isn't always easy, especially when life feels uncertain. But His Word reminds us that His ways are higher than ours, and His plans are for our good. When we surrender control and place our trust in Him, He guides us with wisdom and peace. Let go of your doubts and trust Him fully today.

A PRAYER FOR TRUST

Father, help me to trust You with all my heart and to stop relying on my limited understanding. Teach me to surrender my plans to You and to walk in faith, knowing that You are directing my path. In Jesus' name, Amen.

Your Turn: Reflect on one area of your life where it's hard to trust God.
Write down why it's difficult and what trusting Him would look like for you:

Why It's Hard:

_____

_____

_____

_____

_____

_____

_____

_____

Trusting God means:

By Faith, Declare this:

"

I declare that I trust in God's perfect plan for my life. By faith, I will walk confidently, knowing that He is guiding me every step of the way.

"

Takeaway: This week, when you face uncertainty, pause and declare:
"I trust in God's plan, even when I don't see the whole picture."

Chapter 6: Faith and Trust in God

CHAPTER 7

FAMILY AND RELATIONSHIPS

Are you holding onto bitterness, resentment, or unspoken words that are keeping you from the love God designed for you? What if the peace you've been praying for starts with surrendering that pain to Him?

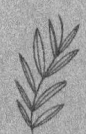

CHAPTER 7

FAMILY AND RELATIONSHIPS

"And above all things have fervent love for one another, for 'love will cover a multitude of sins."
1 Peter 4:8 NKJV

Reflection:

Relationships are a beautiful gift, but they can also be challenging. God calls us to love deeply, forgive freely, and reflect His grace in our interactions. When we seek Him first, He strengthens our relationships and teaches us how to love like Christ. Let Him guide your heart as you navigate the complexities of family and friendships.

A PRAYER FOR RELATIONSHIPS

Lord, thank You for the gift of family and friends. Help me to love others as You have loved me. Teach me to be patient, forgiving, and kind in all my interactions. Strengthen my relationships and fill them with Your peace. In Jesus' name, Amen.

Your Turn: Take a moment to reflect on a relationship in your life that might benefit from God's gentle healing. Consider jotting down ways you can invite Him into that relationship today!

Relationship:

My Prayer for this relationship:

By Faith, Declare this:

I declare that my relationships are strengthened by God's love. By faith, I will reflect His grace and forgiveness in every interaction.

"

Takeaway: This week, focus on showing love in practical ways. Ask God to help you reflect His grace in every interaction.

CHAPTER 8

WISDOM AND DIRECTION

Are you asking God for guidance but still making decisions based on your emotions, fears, or what feels safest? What if wisdom isn't just knowing what to do, but trusting God enough to do it?

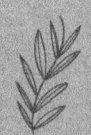

WISDOM AND DIRECTION

"If any of you lacks wisdom, let him ask of God, who gives to all liberally and without reproach, and it will be given to him."
James 1:5 NKJV

Reflection:

In moments of decision, we often feel lost or unsure of the next step. But God promises to give wisdom to those who ask. His guidance is sure, His timing is perfect, and His plans are always good. Trust Him to lead you as you seek His direction for your life.

A PRAYER FOR WISDOM

God, I ask for Your wisdom in every decision I face. Thank You for giving it generously when I ask. Lead me by Your Spirit and help me to trust the paths You place before me. In Jesus' name, Amen.

Your Turn: Think of a decision you need to make. Write down two possible options and ask God to lead you in the right direction:

Option 1:

_____

_____

_____

_____

_____

_____

_____

_____

_____

Option 2:

By Faith, Declare this:

"

I declare that God's wisdom is guiding me in every decision. By faith, I will walk confidently, knowing He is leading me.

"

Takeaway: I declare that God's wisdom is guiding me in every decision. By faith, I will walk confidently, knowing He is leading me.

_____

_____

_____

_____

Chapter 8: Wisdom and Direction

CHAPTER 9

PROVISION AND FINANCIAL PEACE

Do you live like God is your provider, or do you stress over every dollar, every bill, every paycheck? What if real financial peace has nothing to do with how much money you have, but how much trust you place in Him?

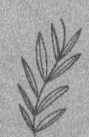

CHAPTER 9

PROVISION AND
FINANCIAL
PEACE

*"And my God shall supply all your
need according to His riches in
glory by Christ Jesus."*
Philippians 4:19 NKJV

Financial stress can weigh heavy on our hearts, but God reminds us that He is our provider. He knows our needs before we ask and promises to supply them according to His riches. Trust Him with your resources and watch Him provide in ways that exceed your expectations.

A PRAYER FOR PROVISION

Father, thank You for being my provider. I trust You to supply all my needs according to Your riches in glory. Help me to steward my resources wisely and to trust You completely in every season. In Jesus' name, Amen.

Your Turn: What is one financial burden you need to release to God? Write it down and pray for His provision in that area:

Burden:

_____

_____

_____

_____

_____

_____

_____

_____

_____

Praying for:

By Faith, Declare this:

"

I declare that God is my provider. By faith, I will not fear lack because He is faithful to meet all my needs.

"

Takeaway: I declare that God is my provider. By faith, I will not fear lack because He is faithful to meet all my needs.

Chapter 9: Provision and Financial Peace

CHAPTER 10

HEALING AND RESTORATION

Is there a wound you've been nursing for years, hoping time would heal it? What if God is asking you to stop covering it up and let Him restore you fully? What would freedom look like for you?

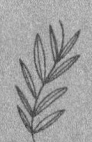

CHAPTER 10

HEALING AND RESTORATION

"He heals the brokenhearted and binds up their wounds."
Psalm 147:3 NKJV

Life brings moments of pain and brokenness, but God is our healer. He restores what has been lost, mends what has been broken, and brings beauty from ashes. Trust Him to work in your heart and life, bringing healing and restoration in His perfect time.

A PRAYER FOR HEALING

Lord, You are my healer. I bring my brokenness to You and ask for Your touch in every wounded place. Restore my heart, renew my strength, and help me to walk in the wholeness You have for me. In Jesus' name, Amen.

Your Turn: Think of one area in your life that needs God's healing. Write a prayer asking Him to restore that part of your heart or life:

My prayer:

_____

_____

_____

_____

_____

_____

_____

_____

_____

By Faith, Declare this:

"

I declare that I am healed and restored in Christ. By faith, I will walk in the fullness of His healing power and grace.

"

Takeaway: This week, meditate on God's ability to heal and restore every broken area of your life.

Chapter 10: Healing and Restoration

CHAPTER 11

PURPOSE AND CALLING

Do you ever feel like you're just going through the motions? What if your purpose isn't about doing more, but about surrendering more to God and letting Him lead you?

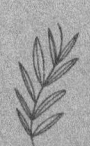

CHAPTER 11

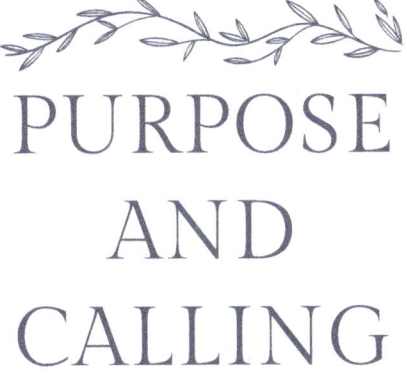

PURPOSE AND CALLING

"For we are His workmanship, created in Christ Jesus for good works, which God prepared beforehand that we should walk in them."
Ephesians 2:10 NKJV

You were created for a purpose. God designed you uniquely and has prepared good works for you to accomplish. When you step into your calling, you reflect His glory and make an eternal impact. Seek Him to reveal His plans and give you the courage to pursue them.

A PRAYER FOR PURPOSE

Father, thank You for creating me with a purpose. Help me see the good works You have prepared for me and to walk boldly in them. Lead me to fulfill the calling You have placed on my life. In Jesus' name, Amen.

Your Turn: What is one step you can take this week toward fulfilling God's purpose for your life? Write it down and commit to acting on it:

Step:

_____

_____

_____

_____

_____

_____

_____

Chapter 11: Purpose and Calling

By Faith, Declare this:

"

I declare that I am walking in God's purpose for my life. By faith, I will fulfill the calling He has placed on me with courage and trust.

"

Takeaway: This week, ask God to reveal one way you can live out His purpose for your life.

_____

_____

_____

_____

Chapter 11: Purpose and Calling

CHAPTER 12

SPIRITUAL GROWTH AND DEVOTION

Have you been coasting in your faith, showing up but not really growing? What's one step you can take today to go deeper with God, even in the middle of your busy life?

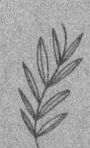

CHAPTER 12

SPIRITUAL GROWTH AND DEVOTION

"But grow in the grace and knowledge of our Lord and Savior Jesus Christ. To Him be the glory both now and forever. Amen."
2 Peter 3:18 NKJV

Reflection:

Spiritual growth is a lifelong journey of drawing closer to God and becoming more like Christ. It requires intentional time in His Word, prayer, and worship. As you devote yourself to knowing Him more, His Spirit will transform you from the inside out.

A PRAYER FOR SPIRITUAL GROWTH

Lord, help me to grow in Your grace and knowledge each day. Teach me to seek You with all my heart and to align my life with Your Word. Transform me into the person You have called me to be. In Jesus' name, Amen.

Your Turn: What is one habit you can develop to grow closer to God? Write it down and commit to it this week:

Habit:

_____

_____

_____

_____

_____

_____

_____

Chapter 12: Spiritual Growth and Devotion

By Faith, Declare this:

"

I declare that I am growing spiritually every day. By faith, I will seek God with all my heart and allow His Word to shape my life.

"

Takeaway: This week, dedicate a specific time each day to grow closer to God through prayer, worship, or Bible study.

_____

_____

_____

_____

_____

Chapter 12: Spiritual Growth and Devotion

CHAPTER 13

BATTLING TEMPTATION AND SIN

What's the one thing you keep struggling with, the thing you tell yourself you'll stop but always seem to return to? What would happen if you stopped trying to fight it alone and truly let God take over?

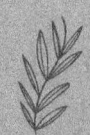

CHAPTER 13

BATTLING TEMPTATION AND SIN

"No temptation has overtaken you except such as is common to man; but God is faithful, who will not allow you to be tempted beyond what you are able, but with the temptation will also make the way of escape, that you may be able to bear it."
1 Corinthians 10:13 NKJV

Reflection:

Temptation is part of life, but God has equipped us with the tools to overcome it. Through His Word, prayer, and the power of His Spirit, we can resist the pull of sin and walk in victory. Trust Him to provide a way out when you face temptation.

A PRAYER FOR STRENGTH AGAINST TEMPTATION

Lord, thank You for Your faithfulness in giving me the strength to resist temptation. Help me to stand firm and choose righteousness. Remind me of the way of escape You provide and give me the courage to take it. In Jesus' name, Amen.

Your Turn: Think of one temptation you face regularly. Write down how you will choose God's way the next time it arises:

Temptation:

_____

_____

_____

_____

_____

_____

_____

God's Way:

By Faith, Declare this:

"

I declare that I am victorious over temptation through Christ. By faith, I will choose God's way in every moment of struggle.

"

Takeaway: This week, memorize:
{1 Corinthians 10:13}
and use it as your weapon against temptation.

Chapter 13: Battling Temptation and Sin

CHAPTER 14

HOPE IN HARD TIME

Have you ever felt like things will never change? Just imagine if God is working behind the scenes in ways you can't quite see yet! Wouldn't you choose to hold onto hope, even when it seems like progress is out of reach?

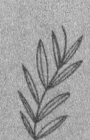

CHAPTER 14

HOPE IN HARD TIMES

"For I know the thoughts that I think toward you, says the Lord, thoughts of peace and not of evil, to give you a future and a hope."
Jeremiah 29:11 NKJV

Hard times can leave us feeling discouraged, but God's plans for us are always filled with hope. He sees the bigger picture and works all things for our good. When we anchor our hope in Him, we can face any challenge with confidence and trust.

 **A PRAYER FOR HOPE**

Father, thank You for being my hope in every season. Remind me of Your plans for my future and grant me the strength to endure when life feels overwhelming. Help me to trust that You are working everything for my good. In Jesus' name, Amen.

Your Turn: What is one promise of God that gives you hope? Write it down and meditate on it this week:

Promise:

_____

_____

_____

_____

_____

_____

_____

_____

God's Way:

By Faith, Declare this:

"

I declare that my hope is in the Lord. By faith, I will trust His plans for my life, even when I don't understand.

"

Takeaway: This week, focus on God's promises and let His hope carry you through every challenge.

Chapter 14: Hope in Hard Times

CHAPTER 15

SURRENDER AND LETTING GO

What are you afraid of losing if you fully surrender to God? Could it be that what you're holding onto is actually holding you back?

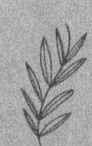

CHAPTER 15

SURRENDER AND LETTING GO

"Cast your burden on the Lord, and He shall sustain you; He shall never permit the righteous to be moved."
Psalm 55:22 NKJV

Letting go isn't a sign of weakness; it's an act of trust. When we surrender our worries, fears, and plans to God, we make space for His peace and guidance. He is strong enough to carry our burdens and faithful enough to sustain us.

A PRAYER FOR SURRENDER

Father, I surrender every worry and burden to You. Teach me to trust Your plan and let go of my need to control. Fill me with peace as I rest in Your care. In Jesus' name, Amen.

Your Turn: What's one thing you need to surrender to God today? Write it down and trust Him with it:

Surrendered to God:

_____

_____

_____

_____

_____

_____

_____

_____

Chapter 15: Surrender and Letting Go

By Faith, Declare this:

"

I declare that I am free from the weight of burdens because I trust in God. By faith, I surrender all to Him and rest in His care.

"

Takeaway: This week, whenever you feel the need to take control, pause and say: *"Lord, I trust You with this."*

Chapter 15: Surrender and Letting Go

CHAPTER 16

WALKING IN FORGIVENESS

Who do you need to forgive, not because they deserve it, but because you deserve to be free? What if your healing is waiting on your willingness to release the pain?

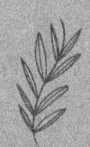

CHAPTER 16

WALKING IN FORGIVENESS

"And be kind to one another,
tenderhearted, forgiving one another,
even as God in Christ forgave you."
Ephesians 4:32 NKJV

Forgiveness is a gift we give ourselves as much as others. Carrying anger and resentment weighs us down, but forgiveness sets us free. Trust God to help you release the hurt and walk in His grace.

A PRAYER FOR FORGIVENESS

Lord, help me to forgive as You have forgiven me. Remove bitterness from my heart and replace it with Your love. Teach me to let go of anger and walk in freedom. In Jesus' name, Amen.

Your Turn: Think of someone you need to forgive. Write their name and ask God for the strength to let go and extend grace:

Name:

_____

_____

_____

_____

_____

_____

_____

_____

_____

Chapter 16: Walking in Forgiveness

By Faith, Declare this:

"

I declare that I am free through forgiveness. By faith, I let go of bitterness and walk in the freedom of God's grace.

"

Takeaway: This week, pray for someone you need to forgive and ask God to heal your heart.

Chapter 16: Walking in Forgiveness

OVERCOMING DOUBT

What falsehoods has the adversary
communicated to you that have
led you to embrace them as truth?
How would your life manifest if you
completely placed your trust in the
sovereignty and character of God?

CHAPTER 17

OVERCOMING DOUBT

"Immediately the father of the child cried out and said with tears, 'Lord, I believe; help my unbelief!'"

Mark 9:24 NKJV

Doubt is something we all face, but it doesn't disqualify us from God's love. He meets us where we are and strengthens our faith when we ask. Lean on Him to overcome doubt and walk confidently in His promises.

A PRAYER FOR FAITH

Lord, when doubt creeps in, help me to believe and trust You fully. Strengthen my faith and remind me of Your faithfulness in every moment of uncertainty. In Jesus' name, Amen.

Your Turn: What's one doubt you struggle with? Write it down and ask God to replace it with faith:

Doubt:

_____

_____

_____

_____

_____

_____

_____

_____

Chapter 17: Overcoming Doubt

By Faith, Declare this:

"

*I declare that my faith is
stronger than my doubt. By faith,
I trust God's promises and rest
in His truth.*

"

Takeaway: This week, meditate on one promise of God that strengthens your faith.

_____

_____

_____

_____

Chapter 17: Overcoming Doubt

CHAPTER 18

JOY IN ALL CIRCUMSTANCES

Is your joy dependent on what's happening around you? What if joy isn't about feeling happy but about knowing that no matter what happens, God is still good?

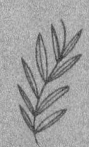

CHAPTER 18

JOY
IN ALL
CIRCUMSTANCES

"Rejoice in the Lord always.
Again I will say, rejoice!"
Philippians 4:4

Reflection:

Joy isn't about what's happening around you; it's about the presence of God within you. Even in hard times, His joy is your strength. Rejoice not in your circumstances but in the unchanging goodness of your Savior.

 **A PRAYER FOR JOY**

Lord, fill my heart with Your joy. Teach me to rejoice in You no matter what I face. Help me to find strength and hope in the joy that comes from Your presence. In Jesus' name, Amen.

Your Turn: What is one reason to rejoice today? Write it down and thank God for it:

Reason to rejoice:

_____

_____

_____

_____

_____

_____

_____

_____

_____

By Faith, Declare this:

"

I declare that my joy comes from the Lord. By faith, I will rejoice in His goodness and let His joy be my strength.

"

Takeaway: This week, choose to rejoice daily by thanking God for one blessing each morning.

_____

_____

_____

_____

_____

Chapter 18: Joy in All Circumstances

FAITHFUL IN WAITING

Are you waiting well, or are you
growing impatient and frustrated?
What if God isn't just making
you wait, but preparing you for
something greater?

CHAPTER 19

FAITHFUL
IN WAITING

"Wait on the Lord; be of good courage,
and He shall strengthen your heart;
wait, I say, on the Lord!"
Psalm 27:14 NKJV

Reflection:

While waiting on God can sometimes feel tough, remember that this is when He truly strengthens us. Trust in His timing and unwavering faithfulness. He's working quietly behind the scenes, preparing wonderful things just for you.

A PRAYER FOR PATIENCE

Lord, teach me to wait on You with courage and trust. Strengthen my heart as I trust Your timing and Your plans for my life. In Jesus' name, Amen.

Your Turn: What are you waiting on God for? Write it down and commit to trusting Him through the process:

Waiting for:

_____

_____

_____

_____

_____

_____

_____

_____

_____

_____

Chapter 19: Faithful in Waiting

By Faith, Declare this:

"

I declare that I am patient in the waiting. By faith, I trust that God's timing is perfect, and His plans are for my good.

"

Takeaway: This week, when impatience rises, pause and pray:
"Lord, I trust Your perfect timing."

Chapter 19: Faithful in Waiting

CHAPTER 20

COURAGE IN FEARFUL TIMES

What fear has been keeping you from stepping into what God has for you? If you knew for a fact that God was backing you up, what would you do differently?

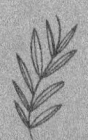

COURAGE IN FEARFUL TIMES

"Have I not commanded you? Be strong and of good courage; do not be afraid, nor be dismayed, for the Lord your God is with you wherever you go."
Joshua 1:9 NKJV

Reflection:

Fear can paralyze us, but God commands us to be strong and courageous. His presence goes with us, giving us the boldness to face any challenge. Trust Him to be your strength during fearful times.

A PRAYER FOR COURAGE

Father, thank You for being with me in every situation. When fear tries to overwhelm me, remind me of Your promise to never leave me. Fill me with courage and strength. In Jesus' name, Amen.

Your Turn: What fear are you facing today? Write it down and declare God's strength over it:

Fear:

_____

_____

_____

_____

_____

_____

_____

_____

Chapter 20: Courage in Fearful Times

By Faith, Declare this:

"

I declare that I am strong and courageous through Christ. By faith, I will face every challenge, knowing that God is with me."

"

Takeaway: This week, confront your fears with God's Word, reminding yourself of Joshua 1:9.

_____

_____

_____

_____

_____

LIVING IN GOD'S GRACE

Do you really believe that God's grace is enough, or are you still trying to prove you're worthy of His love? What if the freedom you've been longing for is found in simply receiving His grace?

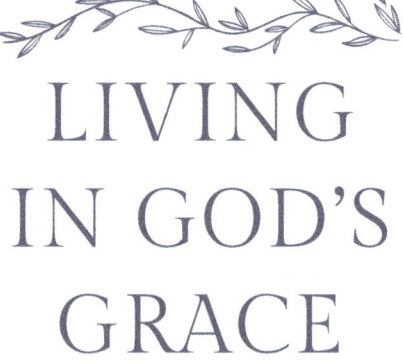

LIVING IN GOD'S GRACE

"And He said to me, 'My grace is sufficient for you, for My strength is made perfect in weakness.'"
2 Corinthians 12:9 NKJV

Reflection:

God's grace isn't something we earn—it's a gift, freely given to us through Christ. His grace covers our failures, strengthens us in our weakness, and empowers us to live boldly for Him. Rest in His grace today, knowing that it's more than enough for every moment.

A PRAYER FOR GRACE

Lord, thank You for Your grace that strengthens me and carries me through each day. Teach me to rest in Your sufficiency and to trust in Your strength in my weakness. In Jesus' name, Amen.

Your Turn: Write down one area where you've seen God's grace at work in your life:

Grace at work:

_____

_____

_____

_____

_____

_____

_____

_____

Chapter 21: Living in God's Grace

By Faith, Declare this:

"

I declare that God's grace is sufficient for me. By faith, I will walk confidently, knowing that His grace covers me in every area of my life.

"

Takeaway: This week, reflect on the moments where God's grace has sustained you and thank Him for it.

Chapter 21: Living in God's Grace

CHAPTER 22

OVERCOMING LONELINESS

Do you feel unseen, forgotten, or like no one truly understands you? What if God is using this season to draw you into a deeper relationship with Him?

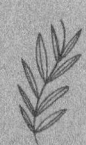

CHAPTER 22

OVERCOMING LONELINESS

"The Lord is near to those who have a broken heart, and saves such as have a contrite spirit."
Psalm 34:18 NKJV

Reflection:

Loneliness can feel overwhelming, but you're never truly alone. God is near to you, even in your most isolated moments. He promises to be your comfort, your friend, and your ever-present help. Lean into His presence and let Him fill the empty spaces in your heart.

A PRAYER FOR GOD'S PRESENCE

Lord, thank You for being near to me when I feel lonely. Remind me of Your constant presence and fill my heart with Your peace and love. In Jesus' name, Amen.

Your Turn: What's one way you can invite God into your lonely moments this week? Write it down:

Invitation to God:

_____

_____

_____

_____

_____

_____

_____

_____

_____

Chapter 22: Overcoming Loneliness

By Faith, Declare this:

"

I declare that God's grace is sufficient for me. By faith, I walk confidently, knowing that His grace covers me in every area of my life.

"

Takeaway: I declare that God's grace is sufficient for me. By faith, I walk confidently, knowing that His grace covers me in every area of my life.

Chapter 22: Overcoming Loneliness

CHAPTER 23

THE POWER OF PRAYER

Can you remember the last time you prayed with boldness, truly believing that God could make your desires a reality? Imagine if the breakthrough you've been longing for is just waiting for you on the other side of a prayer you haven't yet lifted up?

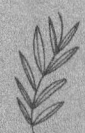

CHAPTER 23

THE POWER
OF PRAYER

"The effective, fervent prayer of a
righteous man avails much."
James 5:16 NKJV

Prayer holds wonderful power as it connects us to the One who has all authority. Through prayer, we can share our burdens, requests, and praises with God, and rest assured that He hears us and responds lovingly. Let's embrace prayer as a daily priority and see how beautifully God works in our lives!

 A PRAYER FOR A DEEPER PRAYER LIFE

Lord, teach me to pray fervently and with faith. Help me to bring everything to You in prayer and to trust in Your perfect timing and will. In Jesus' name, Amen.

Your Turn: Think of one specific area where you want to see God move.

Write it down and commit to praying about it this week:

Prayer focus:

_____

_____

_____

_____

_____

_____

_____

_____

_____

Chapter 23: The Power of Prayer

By Faith, Declare this:

"

I declare that my prayer is my lifeline to God. By faith, I will pray boldly, trusting that my prayers make a difference.

"

Takeaway: This week, set aside dedicated time each day to pray and listen for God's voice.

Chapter 23: The Power of Prayer

FINDING PURPOSE IN PAIN

Have you been wondering why, instead of focusing on what you can do now? What if your pain is part of a powerful story that can help set someone else free?

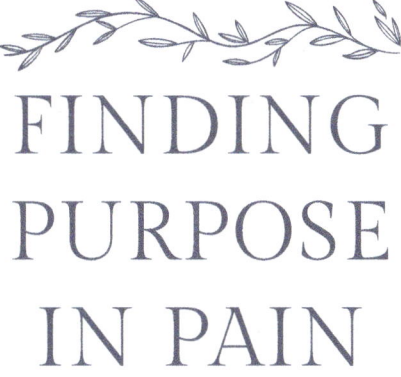

FINDING PURPOSE IN PAIN

"And we know that all things work together for good to those who love God, to those who are the called according to His purpose."
Romans 8:28 NKJV

Pain is never wasted in God's hands. He takes even the hardest moments and uses them to shape us, grow us, and reveal His purpose in our lives. Trust Him to bring beauty from ashes and meaning to your struggles.

A PRAYER FOR PURPOSE

Father, thank You for working all things together for my good. Help me to trust You in my pain and to see Your purpose in every season. In Jesus' name, Amen.

Your Turn: What's one difficult situation where you've seen or hope to see God's purpose revealed? Write it down:

Purpose in pain:

Chapter 24: Finding Purpose in Pain

By Faith, Declare this:

"

I declare that my pain is not wasted. By faith, I trust God to bring purpose and beauty from every struggle.

"

Takeaway: This week, ask God to show you how He is working in your struggles and thank Him for His faithfulness.

Chapter 24: Finding Purpose in Pain

TRUSTING GOD IN TRANSITIONS

Are you afraid of what's next because
you don't know what it will look like?
What if God is already in your next
season, waiting for you to trust Him
to lead you there?

CHAPTER 25

TRUSTING GOD IN TRANSITIONS

"For I know the thoughts that I think toward you, says the Lord, thoughts of peace and not of evil, to give you a future and a hope."
Jeremiah 29:11 NKJV

Transitions can be unsettling, but they're also opportunities to trust God in new ways. Whether you're starting something new or leaving something behind, God's plans for you are good. Trust Him to guide you through every change.

 ## A PRAYER TO TRUST DURING TRANSITIONS

Lord, thank You for holding my future in Your hands. Help me to trust You in every transition and to walk boldly into the plans You have for me. In Jesus' name, Amen.

Your Turn: What's one transition you're navigating right now? Write it down and pray for God's guidance:

Current transition:

_____

_____

_____

_____

_____

_____

_____

_____

_____

_____

Chapter 25: Trusting God in Transitions

By Faith, Declare this:

"

I declare that God is leading me through every transition. By faith, I trust His plans for my future.

"

Takeaway: This week, remind yourself daily that God's plans for you are full of hope and peace.

Chapter 25: Trusting God in Transitions

CHAPTER 26

HOPE FOR THE FUTURE

Do you ever feel a bit uneasy about the unknown, or do you find comfort in trusting that God holds your future? Perhaps the uncertainty you're facing is a gentle reminder to strengthen your faith in Him!

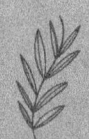

CHAPTER 26

HOPE
FOR THE
FUTURE

*"Now may the God of hope fill you
with all joy and peace in believing,
that you may abound in hope by the
power of the Holy Spirit."*
Romans 15:13 NKJV

Reflection:

Even in uncertainty, God offers us a future filled with
hope. His promises never fail, and His plans are always
good. Trust Him to guide you toward His purpose,
and let hope be the anchor that keeps you steady.

A PRAYER FOR HOPE

Lord, thank You for being the God of hope. Fill my heart with joy and peace as I trust in Your promises for my future. In Jesus' name, Amen.

Your Turn: What's one area where you need hope for the future? Write it down and surrender it to God:

Hopeful Area:

_____

_____

_____

_____

_____

_____

_____

_____

_____

_____

Chapter 26: Hope for the Future

By Faith, Declare this:

"

I declare that my hope is in the Lord. By faith, I trust His plans and look forward to the future with confidence.

"

Takeaway: This week, meditate on God's promises and let His hope fill your heart with peace.

Chapter 26: Hope for the Future

CHAPTER 27

LIVING WITH ETERNAL PERSPECTIVE

Are you living for the present or for what lasts forever? If you knew today was your last, would you be proud of how you spent your time, energy, and love?

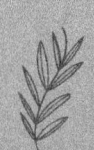

LIVING WITH ETERNAL PERSPECTIVE

"For our light affliction, which is but for a moment, is working for us a far more exceeding and eternal weight of glory."
2 Corinthians 4:17 NKJV

Reflection:

Life on earth is temporary, but eternity is forever. When we focus on what truly matters—God's kingdom and His glory—it shifts our perspective and helps us endure life's challenges with joy and purpose.

 A PRAYER FOR ETERNAL FOCUS

Lord, help me to fix my eyes on the eternal rewards You have prepared. Teach me to live with a perspective that honors You and brings glory to Your name. In Jesus' name, Amen.

Your Turn: What's one way you can shift your focus to eternity this week?

Write it down:

_____

_____

_____

_____

_____

_____

_____

_____

_____

Eternal focus:

By Faith, Declare this:

"

I declare that I will live with eternity in mind. By faith, I will focus on God's kingdom and trust Him to use my life for His glory.

"

Takeaway: This week, remind yourself daily that this life is temporary, but God's promises are eternal.

Chapter 27: Living with Eternal Perspective

CHAPTER 28

RELYING ON GOD'S STRENGTH

Have you been carrying burdens that God never intended for you to bear? What if you stopped trying to be strong on your own and allowed His strength to take over?

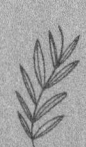

RELYING ON GOD'S STRENGTH

"I can do all things through Christ who strengthens me."
Philippians 4:13 NKJV

Reflection:

God's strength is limitless, and He offers it to us when we feel weak. We don't have to rely on our own abilities or power; instead, we can rest in His strength, which is more than enough to sustain us.

A PRAYER FOR STRENGTH

Lord, thank You for being my source of strength. When I feel weak, remind me that Your power is made perfect in my weakness. In Jesus' name, Amen.

Your Turn: What's one challenge you're facing where you need God's strength? Write it down and pray for His power to sustain you:

Challenge:

Chapter 28: Relying on God's Strength

By Faith, Declare this:

"

I declare that I can do
all things through Christ.
By faith, I will rely on His
strength and not my own.

"

Takeaway: This week, lean on God's strength in every challenge and trust Him to sustain you.

_____

_____

_____

_____

Chapter 28: Relying on God's Strength

CHAPTER 29

THE GIFT OF GRATITUDE

When was the last time you sincerely thanked God—not just for what He has done, but for who He is? What if the joy you've been seeking is waiting on the gratitude you've been holding back?

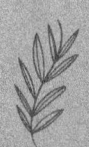

CHAPTER 29

THE GIFT OF GRATITUDE

"In everything give thanks; for this is the will of God in Christ Jesus for you."
1 Thessalonians 5:18 NKJV

Gratitude transforms our perspective, allowing us to see God's blessings even in difficult seasons. When we practice giving thanks in all things, we open our hearts to joy and contentment in His goodness.

 **A PRAYER OF THANKS**

Heavenly Father, thank You for Your countless blessings. Teach me to have a grateful heart and to give thanks in every situation, trusting in Your plan. In Jesus' name, Amen.

Your Turn: Write down three things you're thankful for today and thank God for each of them:

1.

_____

_____

2.

_____

_____

3.

_____

_____

_____

_____

_____

Chapter 29: The Gift of Gratitude

By Faith, Declare this:

"

I declare that I will live with a heart of gratitude. By faith, I will thank God in all things and trust in His goodness.

"

Takeaway: This week, practice daily gratitude by writing down one thing you're thankful for each day.

_____

_____

_____

_____

Chapter 29: The Gift of Gratitude

CHAPTER 30

THE BATTLE OF THE MIND

What thoughts have you allowed to shape your reality—God's truth or the enemy's lies? What if the biggest battle you're facing right now isn't your circumstances, but what you believe about them?

CHAPTER 30

THE BATTLE OF THE MIND

"And do not be conformed to this world, but be transformed by the renewing of your mind, that you may prove what is that good and acceptable and perfect will of God."
Romans 12:2 NKJV

Our minds are a battlefield, and the enemy often attacks us with lies and doubts. But God's Word has the power to renew our minds and transform our thoughts. Meditate on His truth and let it guide you toward His perfect will.

A PRAYER FOR A RENEWED MIND

Lord, renew my mind with Your truth and help me to resist the lies of the enemy. Transform my thoughts to align with Your will and Your Word. In Jesus' name, Amen.

Your Turn: What's one negative thought you need to replace with God's truth? Write it down and counter it with scripture:

Negative Thought:

_____

_____

_____

_____

_____

_____

_____

God's Truth:

_____

_____

_____

_____

_____

_____

_____

_____

_____

_____

_____

_____

_____

_____

_____

_____

_____

By Faith, Declare this:

"

I declare that my mind is renewed by God's Word. By faith, I will think on things that are true, noble, and praiseworthy.

"

Takeaway: This week, when negative thoughts arise, replace them with a scripture that reminds you of God's truth.

Chapter 30: The Battle of The Mind

CHAPTER 31

FAITH THAT MOVES MOUNTAINS

Do you pray with expectation, or do you brace yourself for disappointment? What if the only thing standing between you and your breakthrough is the boldness of your faith?

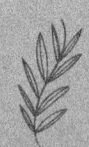

CHAPTER 31

FAITH THAT MOVES MOUNTAINS

"So Jesus said to them, 'Because of your unbelief; for assuredly, I say to you, if you have faith as a mustard seed, you will say to this mountain, "Move from here to there," and it will move; and nothing will be impossible for you."
Matthew 17:20 NKJV

Reflection:

Even the smallest amount of faith, when placed in a limitless God, can do the impossible. Trust in His power and believe that He can move the mountains in your life.

A PRAYER OF FAITH

Lord, thank You for the gift of faith. Strengthen my belief and remind me that nothing is impossible with You. In Jesus' name, Amen.

Your Turn: What's one mountain you need God to move in your life? Write it down and pray for His power to work:

Mountain:

_____

_____

_____

_____

_____

_____

_____

_____

_____

_____

Chapter 31: Faith that Moves Mountains

By Faith, Declare this:

"

I declare that my faith is strong and unwavering. By faith, I trust God to move mountains in my life.

"

Takeaway: This week, boldly believe in the impossible and trust in God's power to move mountains.

_____

_____

_____

_____

_____

Chapter 31: Faith that Moves Mountains

CHAPTER 32

RESTING IN GOD'S TIMING

Are you frustrated with where you are, feeling like God is taking too long? What if His delay is actually His protection? Would you still trust Him even when the timeline doesn't match your plans?

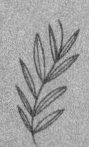

CHAPTER 32

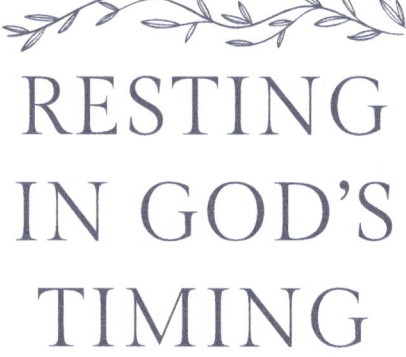

RESTING IN GOD'S TIMING

"He has made everything beautiful in its time."
Ecclesiastes 3:11 NKJV

Reflection:

God's timing is always perfect, even when it feels delayed. Trust that He is working behind the scenes to align every detail for His glory and your good.

A PRAYER FOR PATIENCE

Lord, teach me to wait on You with courage and trust. Strengthen my heart as I trust Your timing and Your plans for my life. In Jesus' name, Amen.

Your Turn: What are you waiting on God for? Write it down and commit to trusting Him through the process:

Waiting for:

_____

_____

_____

_____

_____

_____

_____

_____

_____

Chapter 32: Resting in God's Timing

By Faith, Declare this:

"

I declare that I am patient in the waiting. By faith, I trust that God's timing is perfect, and His plans are for my good.

"

Takeaway: This week, when impatience rises, pause and pray:
"Lord, I trust Your perfect timing."

_____

_____

_____

_____

Chapter 32: Resting in God's Timing

_____

_____

_____

_____

_____

_____

_____

_____

_____

_____

_____

_____

_____

_____

_____

_____

CHAPTER 33

SERVING OTHERS WITH JOY

Do you serve out of obligation, or out of love? What if the joy you're missing isn't in receiving more, but in giving more than you ever have before?

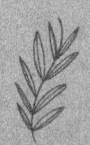

CHAPTER 33

SERVING OTHERS WITH JOY

"For even the Son of Man did not come to be served, but to serve, and to give His life a ransom for many."
Mark 10:45 NKJV

Serving others reflects the heart of Christ. When we serve with joy, we demonstrate His love and bring glory to God.

A PRAYER FOR A SERVANT'S HEART

Lord, teach me to serve others with joy and humility. Help me reflect Your love in my actions and to glorify You through service. In Jesus' name, Amen.

Your Turn: Who is someone you can serve this week? Write down how you will show them Christ's love:

Person:

Act of Service:

By Faith, Declare this:

"

I declare that I will serve others with joy. By faith, I will reflect Christ's love in everything I do.

"

Takeaway: This week, look for opportunities to serve others with joy and humility.

Chapter 33: Serving Others with Joy

CHAPTER 34

STANDING FIRM IN TRIALS

When hard times come, do you find yourself clinging to God or questioning Him? What if this storm isn't meant to break you but to build you into the warrior, He's called you to be?

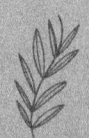

CHAPTER 34

STANDING FIRM IN TRIALS

"Therefore take up the whole armor of God, that you may be able to withstand in the evil day, and having done all, to stand."
Ephesians 6:13 NKJV

Trials test our faith, but they also strengthen it. With God's armor, you can stand firm no matter what comes your way.

A PRAYER FOR STRENGTH IN TRIALS

Father, equip me with Your armor so I can stand firm in every trial. Strengthen me to trust You in the face of adversity. In Jesus' name, Amen.

Your Turn: What's one trial you're facing? Write it down and ask God for His strength to stand firm:

Trial:

_____

_____

_____

_____

_____

_____

_____

_____

_____

_____

_____

Prayer for Strength:

By Faith, Declare this:

"

I declare that I will stand firm in trials. By faith, I will rely on God's strength to overcome every challenge.

"

Takeaway: This week, focus on putting on God's armor daily and trusting Him through trials.

CHAPTER 35

THE JOY OF SALVATION

Do you still carry the same excitement for Jesus that you had when you first gave your life to Him? What if your joy hasn't been lost—only buried beneath distractions that God is calling you to remove?

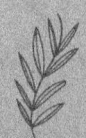

THE JOY OF SALVATION

"Restore to me the joy of Your salvation, and uphold me by Your generous Spirit."
Psalm 51:12 NKJV

Reflection:

Salvation is the greatest gift we can ever receive. Rediscover the joy of knowing you are saved by grace and loved by God.

 **A PRAYER FOR JOY**

Lord, thank You for the gift of salvation. Restore the joy of Your salvation in my heart and help me to live in gratitude. In Jesus' name, Amen.

Your Turn: Write down one way you can celebrate the joy of your salvation this week:

Celebration:

_____

_____

_____

_____

_____

_____

_____

_____

Chapter 35: The Joy of Salvation

By Faith, Declare this:

"

I declare that I am patient in the waiting. By faith, I trust that God's timing is perfect, and His plans are for my good.

"

Takeaway: This week, reflect on the gift of salvation and let it renew your joy.

_____

_____

_____

_____

_____

CHAPTER 36

GOD'S LIGHT IN DARKNESS

Have you been feeling surrounded by darkness, wondering where God is? What if He's been shining all along, but you've been looking in the wrong direction?

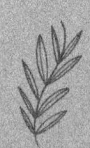

GOD'S LIGHT IN DARKNESS

"The Lord is my light and my salvation; whom shall I fear? The Lord is the strength of my life; of whom shall I be afraid?"
Psalm 27:1 NJKV

Reflection:

Even in the darkest moments, God's light shines to guide us. He is our hope, our strength, and our salvation. Trust Him to illuminate your path and bring clarity to every situation.

 **A PRAYER FOR LIGHT**

Lord, You are my light and salvation. Shine Your light into every dark area of my life and help me to walk boldly in Your truth. In Jesus' name, Amen.

Your Turn: What's one area where you need God's light to shine? Write it down and pray for His guidance.

Dark Area:

_____

_____

_____

_____

_____

_____

_____

_____

Prayer for Guidance:

By Faith, Declare this:

"

I declare that God's light leads me through every darkness. By faith, I will trust Him to guide my path.

"

Takeaway: This week, remember that God's light overcomes any darkness you face.

_____

_____

_____

_____

_____

Chapter 36: God's Light in Darkness

CHAPTER 37

THE PEACE OF SURRENDER

Are you exhausted from trying to control everything in your life? What if the peace you've been craving is waiting on your willingness to let go and trust that God knows what He's doing?

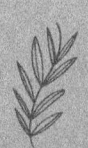

THE PEACE OF SURRENDER

"You will keep him in perfect peace, whose mind is stayed on You, because he trusts in You."
Isaiah 26:3 NKJV

Reflection:

True peace comes when we surrender our lives to God. When we trust Him fully, He replaces our anxieties with His perfect peace.

 **A PRAYER FOR PEACE**

Father, help me to surrender my worries and trust in You. Keep my mind focused on You and fill my heart with Your perfect peace. In Jesus' name, Amen.

Your Turn: What's one worry you can surrender to God today? Write it down and trust Him with it:

Surrendered worry:

Chapter 37: The Peace of Surrender

By Faith, Declare this:

"

I declare that I have perfect peace in God. By faith, I surrender my worries and trust in His plans.

"

Takeaway: This week, practice surrender by giving one specific worry to God each day.

Chapter 37: The Peace of Surrender

CHAPTER 38

WALKING IN BOLDNESS

Are you playing it safe, afraid of stepping into what God has called you to? What if fear is the only thing keeping you from a life that is bigger and bolder than you ever imagined?

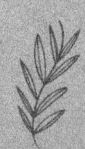

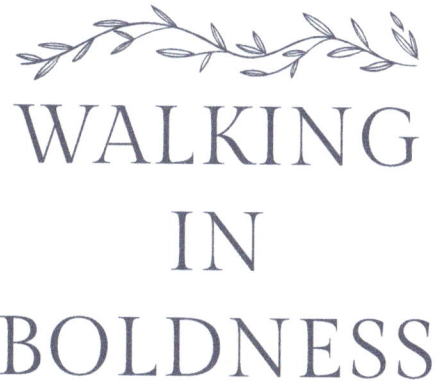

WALKING
IN
BOLDNESS

"The wicked flee when no one pursues,
but the righteous are bold as a lion."
Proverbs 28:1 NKJV

God calls us to walk boldly in faith, trusting in His strength. Whether sharing His Word or standing firm in trials, His Spirit empowers us to live courageously.

 ## A PRAYER FOR BOLDNESS

Lord, fill me with Your boldness and courage. Help me to walk confidently in Your promises and reflect Your love to others. In Jesus' name, Amen.

Your Turn: Where do you need to walk boldly in faith this week? Write it down and pray for courage:

I need to take a step of boldness in the following area(s):

_____

_____

_____

_____

_____

_____

_____

Chapter 38: Walking in Boldness

By Faith, Declare this:

"

I declare that I am bold and courageous in Christ. By faith, I will stand firm and share His truth with confidence.

"

Takeaway: This week, take one step of boldness, trusting that God is with you.

Chapter 38: Walking in Boldness

OVERCOMING COMPARISON

How many times have you looked
at someone else's life and wondered
why you aren't where they are?
What if God's greatest work in you is
happening in the unseen places, in
His perfect way and timing?

CHAPTER 39

OVERCOMING
COMPARISON

*"For we dare not class ourselves or
compare ourselves with those who
commend themselves. But they,
measuring themselves by themselves,
and comparing themselves among
themselves, are not wise."*
2 Corinthians 10:12 NKJV

Reflection:

Comparison steals joy and distracts us from God's
unique purpose for our lives. Focus on His plans for
you and celebrate the gifts He's given you.

 **A PRAYER FOR CONTENTMENT**

Father, thank You for creating me uniquely and for Your plans for my life Help me to find contentment in You and to stop comparing myself to others. In Jesus' name, Amen.

Your Turn: What's one area where you've struggled with comparison? Write it down and ask God to help you trust Him:

Surrendered worry:

_____

_____

_____

_____

_____

_____

_____

_____

Chapter 39: Overcoming Comparison

By Faith, Declare this:

"

I declare that I am content in God's plan for my life. By faith, I will focus on His purpose and celebrate His gifts.

"

Takeaway: This week, focus on gratitude for God's unique plan for your life.

_____

_____

_____

_____

Chapter 39: Overcoming Comparison

CHAPTER 40

RENEWING YOUR SPIRIT DAILY

Are you spiritually drained, running on empty, wondering why you feel disconnected from God? What if the renewal you need isn't a one-time event but a daily decision to seek Him first?

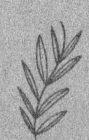

CHAPTER 40

RENEWING YOUR SPIRIT DAILY

"But those who wait on the Lord shall renew their strength; they shall mount up with wings like eagles, they shall run and not be weary, they shall walk and not faint."
Isaiah 40:31 NKJV

Reflection:

Spiritual renewal isn't a one-time event—it's a daily practice of seeking God's presence. Spend time with Him each day and let Him refresh your spirit and strengthen your faith.

 **A PRAYER FOR RENEWAL**

Dear Lord, I seek You for my daily renewal. Please refresh my spirit, strengthen my heart, and guide me as I walk with You each day. In Jesus' name, Amen.

Your Turn: What's one daily habit you can practice to renew your spirit? Write it down and commit to it:

Renewal Habit:

_____

_____

_____

_____

_____

_____

_____

_____

Chapter 40: Renewing Your Spirit Daily

_____

_____

_____

_____

_____

_____

_____

_____

_____

_____

_____

_____

_____

_____

_____

_____

_____

_____

By Faith, Declare this:

"

I declare that my spirit is renewed daily by God's presence. By faith, I will seek Him and find strength in Him.

"

Takeaway: This week, dedicate time each day to connect with God and renew your spirit.

_____

_____

_____

_____

FINAL THOUGHTS

As you close this book, know that the journey doesn't end here. God's grace, peace, and love are with you every day, guiding you through every challenge and celebration. Keep leaning into Him, trusting His Word, and walking in His truth.

My prayer for you is that you continue to find strength in God, joy in His presence, and peace in His promises. May this book serve as a reminder of His unfailing love and a source of encouragement as you grow in faith.

"The Lord bless you and keep you; the Lord make His face shine upon you and be gracious to you; the Lord lift up His countenance upon you, and give you peace."

(Numbers 6:24-26) NKJV

In Christ's Everlasting Love,

Whitney Ramos

YOUR NEXT STEP

This book is just the beginning of your journey. God is continually working in your life, and there's always more to discover, trust, and surrender to Him. Take the next step in deepening your relationship with Him and sharing His love with others.

Here are some ways you can continue growing:

- **Reflect:** Spend time journaling your thoughts and prayers as you work through what God is teaching you.

- **Share:** Encourage a friend by gifting this book or sharing your favorite chapter with someone who needs it.

- **Connect:** Join a Bible study group or connect with a community of believers for accountability and encouragement.

- **Explore More:** Visit whitneyramos.com for additional resources, devotionals, and encouragement to help you stay connected to God.

"And let us consider one another in order to stir up love and good works."

(Hebrews 10:24) NKJV

May the Lord God bless you richly as you continue walking in His grace and love.

www.ingramcontent.com/pod-product-compliance
Lightning Source LLC
Chambersburg PA
CBHW071720120626
46550CB00001B/319